PROCESS THEOLOGY AND THE REVIVAL WE NEED

BRUCE G. EPPERLY

Topical Line Drives, #52

Energion Publications
Gonzalez, Florida
2023

ISBN: 978-1-63199-867-6
eISBN: 978-1-63199-868-3

Energion Publications
PO Box 841
Gonzalez, FL 32560

https://energion.com
pubs@energion.com

TABLE OF CONTENTS

1	Revival, Revolution, Or Reaction	1
2	A Personal Relationship With Jesus in a Process-Relational World	14
3	Charismatic Cosmopolitanism	24
4	Why Not Become Fire?	31
5	A Moving Image Of Eternity	37
	Books For The Revival We Need	42

CHAPTER ONE

REVIVAL, REVOLUTION, OR REACTION

Revive us again - fill each heart with thy love;
May each soul be rekindled with fire from above.
Hallelujah, Thine the glory, Hallelujah, Amen
Hallelujah, Thine the glory, Revive us again...[1]

> The worship of God is not a rule of safety – it is an adventure of spirit, the flight after the unattainable. The death of religion comes with the repression of the high hope of adventure.[2]

On Sunday, November 1, 1970, I came home to Jesus. I didn't die and go to heaven. But, I found God. I experienced the joy of God's nearness and a faith I could believe in. It was an improbable return to a faith that I had abandoned as an early teen. A remarkable reentry to companionship with the Jesus of my evangelical childhood. Two weeks before on October 17, I took a bus from San Jose, California, to Berkeley, where I learned Transcendental Meditation, a Hindu spiritual practice tailored to the lifestyles of Westerners. I received my "personal mantra," was counseled to meditate twice daily, and sent back to college with a new spiritual vision. I was revived in body, mind, and spirit!

I didn't know it at the time but learning TM changed everything. I was a first-year college student, a month short of my eighteenth birthday. I was a spiritual seeker, and for the previous three years, I had sought union with God through a cocktail of American Transcendentalism, Hindu philosophy, Carlos Castaneda, and weekly doses of LSD supplemented by daily mind expansion with grass and hashish. Psychedelics and global spirituality changed my life, but I felt the lure to something more. I knew that my spiritual quest with psychedelics had reached its culmination, and I could go no further on the Magical Mystery

---

1 W.P. Mackay, "Revive Us Again" (1863).
2 Alfred North Whitehead, *Science and the Modern World* (New York: Free Press, 1997), 192.

Tour, without depleting mind, body, and spirit. When I saw the placards, announcing TM classes at San Jose State, I believed that I had found a way to wholeness, peace of mind, and experiencing God.

Two weeks later, I returned to Grace Baptist Church, adjacent to the campus. Grace was in the process of change at the time. The Vietnam War was in full throttle, and thousands of my contemporaries found themselves fighting for their lives in rice fields, uncertain of the reason, but unwilling to disobey our nation's leaders. George L. "Shorty" Collins, the Baptist College Chaplain, was at the heart of the Bay Area anti-war movement. An old school social gospeler, legendary in the peace movement, nicknamed "Shorty," because he was 6 foot, 7 inches, Shorty protested silently in front of the Bank of America building each Thursday noon and counseled hundreds of young men, including me, seeking "conscientious objector" status. John Akers, the Senior Pastor was on his own spiritual journey in quest for an "adequate theology." They welcomed me and saw the theological and spiritual seeker in me. They gave a long-haired, scraggly bearded, hippie kid a place to call home, a place called Grace. Two years later, John Akers and I took a class together at San Jose State on Process Theology, taught by Richard Keady, a student of John Cobb, and I've never looked back. I found a theology and an emerging spiritual path that keeps evolving and expanding.

REVIVAL AND REVOLUTION

On February 8, 2023, the Asbury Revival emerged without warning, when a group of students felt called to stay after the regular weekly chapel service to continue in prayer and worship. Touched by the Spirit, they prayed, sang, confessed, and worshipped together. What began as an unplanned time of prayer at Asbury University in Western Kentucky became national news, filling the university chapel, and being touted as the beginning of a national revival and return to Christ.[3] Ecstatic, students claimed

---

3 For a first-hand look at the Asbury Revival, see Sojourner Film's "Asbury Outpouring" documentary – "Asbury Outpouring (aka Asbury Revival) | Documentary Film - YouTube"

healing, reconciliation, and a closer walk with Jesus. Not a word about justice or social change, from the many testimonies I heard.

A week later, "The Jesus Revolution," the story of the coming together of the Jesus People, or Jesus Freaks, including Lonnie Frisbee, and Chuck Smith, founder of Calvary Chapel, in Orange Country, California, who welcomed long-haired, non-institutional hippie Christians into his rather staid fundamentalist church, was released in movie theaters. Lonnie Frisbee experienced God's call in the midst of an LSD trip, when he visualized "a vast sea of people crying out to the Lord for salvation, with Frisbee in front preaching the gospel." Mysticism – albeit, drug-induced – led to mission, and the birth of the Calvary Chapel and Vineyard movements. Charismatic, Lonnie Frisbee felt the Spirit release power for spiritual transformation. Spirit-centered, and not primarily doctrinal, Frisbee eventually split from Smith. Later Frisbee was denounced by his former spiritual comrades for his homosexuality. Although he believed homosexuality was a sin, Frisbee typically partied on Saturday night and then preached the gospel on Sunday morning. Frisbee died of AIDS-related complications in 1993.[4]

While many of my Christian friends rejoiced in the Asbury Revival and release of the Jesus Revolution, seeing them as signs of a new spirit that would sweep America, returning the United States to its "Christian roots," many of my Progressive Christian friends dismissed the Asbury Revival as "spirituality lite", puppy love with Jesus, an emotional high, sound and fury signifying nothing spiritually important, and perhaps dangerous if their evangelical experience became coopted by American individualism, conservative politics, and ethical judgmentalism.

The same contrasting responses emerged in relationship to the "Jesus Revolution." On the one hand, many touted it as a harbinger of revival, God's instrument to bring people to Christ. On the other hand, many mourned that youthful, unbridled spiritual idealism was subverted by the doctrinal, exclusivist, and judgmental religion of conservative Christianity. They saw the film as just another

---

4   For more on Lonnie Frisbee, see "Frisbee: The Life and Death of a Hippie Preacher." - "Frisbee: The Life and Death of a Hippie Preacher (2005) - IMDb"

example of the individualistic, anti-LGBTQ+, and socially divisive Christianity that Progressives must condemn.

During the time of this "revival," I had the great joy of attending the Fiftieth Anniversary Celebration of the Center for Process Studies. I pondered the relationship between the cerebral and cosmic process vision, articulated at the conference, and the experiences that give rise to religious movements, including the Jesus movement and Asbury Revival. I wondered if process theology had a role in bridging the gap between mind, body, and spirit, spirituality and intellectuality, and personal faith and global consciousness. Would process theology, in the future, be just another "liberal" movement, scorning mysticism and religious experience, the transpersonal and transrational, in favor of theological correctness and social transformation? Or, would process theology inspire spiritual passion, grounded in holistic theology, to transform the world? Will process theology exemplify "God's frozen chosen" or "become fire," illuminating and energizing contemplative and evangelical spirituality, and promoting a spiritually grounded activism joining inner and outer, faith and action, and personal faith and world loyalty for the healing of the earth? What would I have to contribute to the creative transformation of process theology as a movement to heal the planet and its people?

"WHAT IF?"

When Lonnie Frisbee found his calling to be a messenger of Jesus, this hippie seeker found a path with a heart. He had been looking for God in the study of world religions, UFOs, hypnotism, and psychedelics. He also regularly read the Bible while tripping on LSD. When Frisbee found Jesus, he also found Chuck Smith, a Pentecostal preacher who mentored him and gave him an opportunity to become a Bible study leader. The rest is "history" in charismatic, church growth, and evangelical circles.

Yet, sadly, many idealistic, Jesus-loving young Christians discovered a theological and ethical "bait and switch" in the fundamentalist and charismatic churches they joined. The loving Jesus, who welcomed sinners and outcasts, was supplanted by the stern and legalistic God of biblical literalism, who excluded people of

4

other faiths from salvation, damned the LGBTQ+ community, connected premarital sex and homosexuality with natural disasters, saw AIDS as divine punishment, and abandoned earth care in favor of a constantly updated Second Coming. The authoritarian God of fundamentalist preachers inspired authoritarian cult-like leadership and interpretation of scripture, even among members of the once free-spirited Jesus movement. Questioning church leadership was punished by ostracism and exclusion. The freedom of Jesus' good news gave way to the prison of authoritarian and legalistic religion, eventually driving many Jesus freaks out of the church. Some have left Christianity altogether. Others clung to the Jesus of the summer of love but have no use for institutions. Still others sought a loving and welcoming vision of God and the way of Jesus to deepen and strengthen their relationship to the One who called them by name, forgave their sins, and filled their hearts with love. Ironically, others are now at the forefront of Christian nationalism, racism, and homophobia.

As I look at the life of Lonnie Frisbee, I wonder, "What if Frisbee had found a liberal pastor to partner with? What if a liberal spiritual leader, open to mystical experiences, had mentored Frisbee with an open-spirited theology, focused on God's love, and the universality of revelation and Christ's presence, rather than the end-times, exclusivist, fundamentalist theology of Chuck Smith? What if Frisbee had found a pastor who accepted his homosexuality, helped him come out of the closet, and find a path that allowed him to live with integrity as a gay Christian? What if a progressive pastor had asked Frisbee to explore critically and prayerfully the message of his psychedelic Jesus and the mission he had been given?"

Of course, in 1968, homosexuality was still in the closet even in liberal churches, most of whose leaders neither understood nor fully affirmed the varieties of healthy human sexuality. The liberalism of the sixties was primarily political and had little use for mystics and charismatics, judging mysticism as escape from this-worldly issues of war, sexism, racism, and injustice. The majority of liberal pastors had been educated to minimize the transpersonal and non-rational aspects of faith. Their Jesus was primarily a moral teacher and prophet, and not a mystic and healer. They judged mystics as other-worldly and politically irrelevant. They were also taught to see the healings of Jesus as legends from a bygone era. Anyone who turns on an electric light, as Rudolf Bultmann suggested, must deny any form of miracle, including the healings that were at the heart of Jesus' ministry. Perhaps, according to the liberal theology of the sixties, God made a difference in the world, and prayer had some impact on our lives, but the real work of being a Christian involved social activism. Lacking a world view describing God's intimate presence and activity in the universe and our lives, most sixties liberals embraced a type of deism, in which humankind was the primary agent in historical change and God was left at the sidelines to observe our efforts.

I am sure that Lonnie Frisbee's mysticism and sense of calling would have been quite different had he been welcomed into a mainstream or liberal progressive congregation that provided spiritual guidance and mentoring in the development of his spiritual gifts and understanding the meaning of his mystical sense of vocation. Perhaps, he would have discovered a more egalitarian approach to ministry and a faith that helped him integrate his sexuality and sense of call with the ethical standards necessary for healthy congregational leadership.

A Progressive Welcome.

A few years after Frisbee's psychedelic call to ministry, I returned to the church. I am a theologian, pastor, and spiritual teacher today as the result of the hospitality and mentoring I received from a progressive Baptist congregation and its two pastors. Despite my long hair, countercultural lifestyle, and experience with psychedelics, I was given the opportunity to grow into leadership, study process theology with the Senior Pastor, and embark on my teaching career, leading classes as a college student on John Cobb's *God and the World* and Whitehead's *Religion in the Making*.

Unlike Frisbee, I did not claim a mandate from God. I was simply living out a growing sense of vocation, sharing my theological gifts with persons in the congregation. I was also given the opportunity to lead worship at a local nursing home. Still very much a hippie, I shared leadership with another student, Sue Merritt, and

6

learned what it meant to be a pastor, sharing my understanding of God's vision as a pastor to promote the spiritual wellbeing of a small community of convalescent home residents. At Grace Baptist, I took the first steps of a journey of over fifty years joining theological reflection, pastoral leadership, and mystical experience. I found a lifelong path with a heart in process-relational theology.

Progressive and Process and Relational Christianity at a Crossroads.

One of my first forays into John Cobb's theology was *Liberal Christianity at the Crossroads*. I was a junior in college and had just finished *Is it Too Late?* and *God and the World*. I was a budding process theologian, planning to apply to Claremont Graduate School to study with John Cobb. I was active in a liberal congregation and was beginning to recognize the gifts and limitations of the liberal Christian tradition. Liberal Christians were, as Cobb notes in his book, strong on openness to culture, but we were also, as my life-long mentor intuited, distancing ourselves from the vital spiritual roots of Christian faith.

In the progressive and process-relational theology I claimed as a college student, we explored new images of God as companion, actively present and responsive to joy and suffering of history. God was embedded in our lives, working within the concreteness of everyday life and history. The relationally powered God did not predestine or control the present or the future. Rather, the future was open for both God and us. If our planet was to survive, we needed the grace and wisdom of God, and the omni-active Energy of Love. Conversely, God needed our companionship to tip the scales of the moral and spiritual arcs of history toward justice and planetary flourishing. What we do matters, not just to one another and the planet, but also to God. Finite and fallible, we are history makers and planet shapers, and in good measure, the future is in our hands. Yet, progressive and process theologians struggled with personally experiencing God and taking prayer or survival after death seriously in the maelstrom of social activism. Sometimes we were more certain of what we didn't believe, and wanted to condemn, in the old-time religion, than what we believed in terms of prayer and the role of Jesus in our lives. Despite the influx of Buddhist and Hindu spiritual teachers in North America in the sixties, there were few liberal Christians prepared to mentor us in prayer and meditation.

Fifty years have passed since I first encountered *Liberal Christianity at the Crossroads,* and process-relational theology and progressive Christianity are still at a crossroads in finding our spiritual rootedness in a changing cultural context. In 1973, Cobb's concern was an apparently rudderless church and social order in the wake of the Vietnam War. If anything, the liberal or progressive church has been pushed further to the margins in the past fifty years and is on the verge of becoming spiritually and culturally irrelevant even to its members. The American ship of state is being torn apart by waves of white nationalism, racism, violence, incivility, and factionalism, placing the soul of the nation is in jeopardy. Progressive congregations struggle to reclaim their members after two years of worship on Zoom. Many may never come back to in-person worship and fellowship, preferring bagels and coffee or wine and cheese in the comfort of their homes while streaming services at their leisure.

The church as we knew it in 2020 will never come back. Although we believe God is in the process, and God's work involves change, anxiety about the future is overwhelming in many progressive congregations. We struggle to believe that new and creative adventures lie ahead for progressive churches. Literally and figuratively, we need a "come to Jesus" moment. We need a spiritual and theological revival! Not a revival that deconstructs, or destroys, progressive churches, but one that heals, transforms, and awakens progressive Christians to the to lively integration of mysticism, spirituality, and social transformation.

Process theology is at the crossroads. Process thought has gone global and is making inroads in the Peoples Republic of China, and this is good news as in our quest for environmental sustainability. Process and Faith, the primary online platform for process theological reflection, has expanded beyond its initial Christian focus to become "a multi-faith network for relational spirituality and the common good," grounded in the core values of whole persons, whole communities, whole planet, and holistic thinking. The Christian path is now one of nineteen paths affirmed by the Process and Faith online community. This is also good news for global-spirited Christians. Still, Christian process theologians must articulate our own vision of wholeness and healing of persons and the planet, not to mention holistic thinking and spirituality in the church. With the decline of the impact of process theology, or any theology, in seminaries, those of us who claim to be Christian process theologians and spiritual leaders must find innovative and effective ways to promote holistic, spiritually vital, and practical visions of Christianity in partnership with academic theologians. We must reclaim, revive, repair, and revolutionize the spiritual center of Christian faith to expand its impact on our congregants, communities, nation, and planet. We must truly embrace a constructive vision grounded in the interplay of theology, spirituality, and personal and social transformation.

One of my theological mentors, David Griffin predicted that the twenty-first century would be the Whiteheadian century. While that promise has yet to be achieved, it is clear that, within the Christian community, the future of process theology depends on a revival and realization of "whole persons, whole communities, a whole planet, and holistic thinking" that involves the interplay of contemplation and action, and head, heart, and hands. Process theologians and followers need to be open to continuous revival inspired by a living, companioning, energizing, and possibility-giving God, who makes a way toward the future when we see no way forward. We need to reclaim the transformative mission of Jesus.

My use of the word "revival" in the same sentence with process theology and progressive Christianity may seem out of place. When most of us think of revival, we visualize rallies with people walking forward to a stage, and persons enthralled by saccharine hymns or deafening praise bands. We image tears and pleas to accept "Jesus as your personal savior." This bombastic religiosity is foreign to most process theologians and progressive Christian's experience and perhaps with good reason. In contrast, I see "revival" as the emergence of deep and passionate spirituality that changes us and the world, grounded in reclaiming of Jesus as a companion, challenger, and guide. A transformed vision in which God calls persons and communities to partnership in healing their lives, relationships, and the planet. Revival is creative transformation that heals body, mind, and spirit, energizes us, and sends us out in the world as "mystics in action," loving God in the world of the flesh and healing the world God loves. God is alive, God speaks to us, and God challenges us to push forward the moral and spiritual arcs of history.

A Personal Word

This text arose out of my personal commitment to progressive Christianity and the vocation of process theology to provide an open-spirited theological, spiritual, ethical, and missional path for the spiritual and moral future of persons, congregations, and planet. I believe that process theology's vision of reality undergirds transformational commitment to the healthy and life-affirming diversity, pluralism, spirituality, and social and economic justice necessary for our planet's survival.

With Martin Luther King, I believe that the progressive church, influenced by a process-relational world view, should be a head light and not a taillight in response to the critical social, political, ethical, and planetary issues of our time. Our democracy and planet are in peril and need the cosmopolitan, justice-seeking, and earth-affirming voice of process theology. While I cannot predict the contours of the progressive and process Christianity of the future, I believe that process theology must be liberated from the academy to transform Christianity and the world. I am a professor, academic, pastor, and spiritual guide. I also realize that the futures of academic process theology and progressive Christianity are intertwined in their vocation to heal the earth. The future of process-relational theology depends on joining theory and practice, and contemplation and action, and the commitment to share good news beyond the academy.

My hope is that the young people experiencing the Asbury Revival and others like them will join their ecstatic experiences with theologies that embrace spiritual practices, earth care, and God's wondrous diversity of race and sexuality. My prayer is that their experience of Jesus be global and hospitable, not parochial

10

and judgmental. To be a "fountain flowing deep and wide" and not a scant trickle for Christians only, shallow and narrow.

This book is personal. I did not "choose" to write it. I had just finished a trilogy of short books on process theology and mysticism, healing, and prophetic faith, and was planning to take a rest from my vocation as a writer, letting new thoughts and directions have an opportunity to emerge gradually and shape the future as I navigate my seventh decade.

One morning, as I was taking my predawn walk through my Potomac, Maryland, suburb, I was reflecting on a thread of online conversation about the Jesus Revolution and Asbury Revival posted by friends and colleagues on the Advisory Team for the Christian Path of Process and Faith. Their concerns, critiques, and affirmations of these religious experiences resonated with me. I felt that they provided a pathway for conversation and action for "just such a time as this." I felt an inner stirring, drawing me to reflect seriously on what a holistic spiritual revival might mean for progressive Christians and process theologians. I felt a sense of divine inspiration, guiding my steps as a writer, who hoped to have something to contribute to the wellbeing of our planet, process theology, and my nation.

As I make this small contribution to process-relational revival, I am grateful for those who nurtured me: my evangelical Baptist pastor-father Everett Epperly; my spiritually faithful, mother Loretta Baxter Epperly; the pastors whose hospitality guided my first steps in ministry, John Akers and Shorty Collins; and the teachers who introduced and nurtured my expertise in process theology, Marie Fox, Richard Keady, John Cobb, David Griffin, and Bernard Loomer, and to my Claremont classmates and members of the Process and Faith Christian Path Advisory Team. A theologian without love is a "noisy gong and a clanging cymbal" and so I dedicate this book to my companion of over forty-five years, Kate, my son Matt and his wife Ingrid, and my two grandsons Jack and James, whose future inspires me to do something beautiful for God every day.

EMBRACING THE REVIVAL WE NEED

The revival we need to transform process theology and progressive Christianity and respond to the needs of spiritual seekers within and beyond the church involves awakening to joy, passion, and experiences of the Holy. While God's loving presence precedes and undergirds all our efforts, we can open ourselves to divine grace through spiritual practices. Our theology can be inspired and embodied. We can experience God's nature and presence in the world. We also need to experience Jesus as our empathetic companion and source of possibility, healing, and energetic love.

In words that anticipated Joseph Campbell's counsel to "follow your bliss," contemplative activist Howard Thurman, the author of perhaps the first Black Liberation theology *Jesus and the Disinherited*, counseled: "Don't ask what the world needs. Ask what makes you come alive, and go do it. Because what the world needs is people who have come alive." Two thousand years earlier, Paul of Tarsus, the Christ-intoxicated mystic-evangelist, advised the Christian community at Philippi:

> Rejoice in the Lord always; again I will say, Rejoice. Let your gentleness be known to everyone. The Lord is near. Do not be anxious about anything, but in everything by prayer and supplication with thanksgiving let your requests be made known to God. And the peace of God, which surpasses all understanding, will guard your hearts and your minds in Christ Jesus. (Philippians 4:4-7)

Recognizing the power of passion and joy to transform persons and institutions, this first spiritual practice begins with a time of silence in which you open to experience the "still, small voice" of God with each breath. When you feel spiritually centered, consider the following questions:

- Where are you experiencing God's joy or as the protagonist of "Chariots of Fire," Eric Liddle asserts, feeling "God's pleasure?"
- What makes you come alive – spiritually, emotionally, physically, intellectually, relationally, politically?

12

- What stands in the way of your experiencing God's passion and the abundant and adventurous life God imagines for you?
- What might awaken you to God's vision of possibilities and energy of creative transformation?

In conclusion, give thanks for God's companionship in joy, suffering, and challenge. Affirm gratefully God's love for you and the world, and the open future God seeks for you, your congregation, and the world.

> *Lively God, who rejoices and suffers with us, attune my spirit to your Spirit so that I might embody your incarnation in my life and the world. Filled with a holy passion for possibility, let my light shine and spirit glow to bring healing and wholeness to this good earth. In the Name and Spirit of Jesus our Companion and Challenger. Amen.*

Chapter Two

A Personal Relationship with Jesus in a Process-Relational World

O Master, let me walk with thee
In lowly paths of service free; tell me thy secret;
Help me bear the strain of toil, the fret of care...
In hope that sends a shining ray
Far down the future's broadening way;
In peace that God alone can give,
With thee, O Master, let me live.[5]

> The essence of Christianity is the appeal to the life of Christ as a revelation of the nature of God and of his agency in the world...The Mother, the Child, and the bare manger: the lowly man, homeless and self-forgetful, with his message of peace, love, and sympathy: the suffering, the agony, the tender words as life ebbed, the final despair: and the whole with the authority of supreme victory.[6]

During the summer of 1962, I accepted Jesus as my personal Savior. Leonard Eilers, cowboy evangelist to the stars, sporting chaps, spurs, jeans, and a white ten-gallon hat, regaled our Baptist church with stories of celebrities, souls saved, lives changed, marriages healed, and deliverance from demon rum. As he sang his marque song, the "Roundup for God", I came forward to claim publicly my identity as a Christian:

Put your foot in the stirrup
Climb onto the horse
The roundup for God is on.

Jesus had been real for me as a child. I felt Jesus as my companion as I tramped along the Salinas River or on my way to school.

---

5   Washington Gladden, "O Master, Let Me Walk with Thee." (1879)
6   Alfred North Whitehead, *Adventures in Ideas* (New York: Free Press, 1967), 167.

I knew Jesus "walked with me and talked with me and told me I was his own."[7] But, on that hot summer night in 1962, as a nine-year-old, I made my formal commitment to Christ. My sins were forgiven and I was bound for heaven.

A few years later, I left the church, driven away by my father's dismissal as pastor of my childhood church, narrow theology, and the lure of the summer of love. I found spiritual guidance in Transcendentalism, Herman Hesse, Hindu and Buddhist scriptures, and psychedelic adventures. After I learned Transcendental Meditation and returned to a progressive form of Christianity, I buried both my evangelical and psychedelic experiences to pursue a rational and thoughtful Christianity, and low temperature mysticism.

Eighteen years, almost to the day from my childhood conversion experience, I kneeled, on June 1, 1980, as Pastor Clayton Gooden, my father Everett, church leaders, and local pastors laid hands on me as I was ordained at Saguaro Christian Church (Disciples of Christ), Tucson, Arizona. That Sunday, I chose as my ordination hymn, "O Master, Let Me Walk with Thee." I wanted to serve Jesus in the church and academy. I committed myself to spiritual leadership in the way of Jesus, asking God to:

Help me the slow of heart to move
By some clear winning word of love;
Teach me the wayward feet to stay,
And guide them in the homeward way.
Teach me thy patience; still with thee
In closer, dearer company,
In work that keeps faith sweet and strong,
In trust that triumphs over wrong.[8]

Although my theology and spirituality have evolved since my ordination, the importance of Jesus as companion and guide and the inspiration of process theology in shaping my ethics, professional life, and world view still centers my faith. I have sought to be open to a continuous process of conversion and creative transformation personally and professionally. Once buried in the closet,

7 Austin Miles, "In the Garden." (1913)
8 "O Master, Let Me Walk with Thee."

I have unearthed the feeling tones and intimacy of a childhood personal relationship of Jesus and the imaginative spiritual flights of the magical mystery tours of my youth. I have come to realize that for me, growing in wisdom and stature, or in S-I-Z-E, as Bernard Loomer says, involves claiming the totality of my spiritual journey, finding a home for contrasting experiences, and opening to God's energy of love and healing in the present moment.

Encountering the Living Jesus. I have ministerial standing in both the Christian Church (Disciples of Christ) and the United Church of Christ (UCC). An ongoing joke among UCC pastors is that the abbreviation UCC means "Unitarians Considering Christ." Like all humor, there is some truth in the comment. Progressive Christians struggle not only with Christ but also with Jesus, theologically and ethically. We aren't particularly "Jesus-y," to use the language of Anne Lamott. We tend to focus on "God," to the neglect of embodied Jesus and the Holy Spirit. We certainly don't want the Jesus touted by the fundamentalist church down the road!

In contrast, I believe that a vital process and progressive theology must revive its focus on Jesus, the Christ, as central to our spirituality and ethics. Focusing on Jesus as a living reality in our lives does not detract from interfaith relationships, but deepens them as we respond from the spiritual and historical center of our faith. A Christ-centered faith revives persons and congregations and sets us loose to transform the world.

John Cobb once stated that Christ, the principle of creative transformation, is the way that excludes no way. The same applies to Jesus of Nazareth. The mystic, teacher, healer, prophet, and resurrected Jesus is both unique and invitational. A "thin place," where the divine and human meet with intensity and transparence, Jesus is fully alive, fully attentive to God, and fully incarnational of God's wisdom. Jesus' divinity is the paradigm and revelation of God's presence in the world, and not a supernatural exception. While progressives and process theologians can sit loose on literal understandings of the virgin birth and bodily resurrection, we can also admit, in the spirit of theologian H. Richard Niebuhr that in a trillion galaxy universe, philosophers err more in what they deny

16

than what they affirm. Jesus is often better understood by mystics, healers, and prophets than horizontally oriented biblical scholars.

All is miracle in a process-relational universe. God's energy of love and wisdom is present in each moment of experience. The whole earth declares God's glory, as Isaiah discovered in his mystical experience in the Jerusalem Temple. Some moments, Christological in nature, declare what it means to be fully alive, and inspire us to embody the energy of incarnation and resurrection in confronting personal and political challenges.

In Jesus, the Infinite Christ joins finite creation and ongoing history to transform the world. "The world lives by the incarnation of God," so claims Alfred North Whitehead, and our experience of God's incarnational power varies from moment to moment. Jesus as the Christ can be seen as the most dramatic expression of God's vision, reflecting both divine agency and human response in one seamless spiritual experience. The incarnation of God in Jesus awakens us to God's lively incarnation in our own lives, in prayer and compassionate personal and social action. In centering on the life of Jesus and invoking Jesus' name in our daily lives, worship, and social action, we claim Jesus' energy, power, and transformational love in our time and place. Jesus as Christ is not bound to time or place but lives on as a field of force and loving energy, shaping the first and twenty-first-century worlds, and awakening the energies of healing and spiritual transformation. In invoking Jesus' name and awakening to his wisdom and power, we share more fully in his living presence and discover the meaning of Jesus' promise, we "can do greater things" in our spiritual, relational, and political lives. In centering on Jesus, "saying his name," he comes alive as a contemporary force for creative transformation in our world.[9]

Following Jesus. One of my favorite hymns has its origins in India, testifying both to the cost of discipleship and the joys of companionship with the Living Jesus.

I have decided to follow Jesus;
I have decided to follow Jesus;

9 For more on Jesus' presence in our lives and the world, see Epperly, *Messy Incarnation: Meditations on Christ in Process* (Energion, 2022).

I have decided to follow Jesus;
No turning back, no turning back.

Claiming Jesus as Companion, Challenger, Healer, and Savior, leads to a life of continuous creative transformation in which we are no longer conformed to this world, but transformed by the renewing of our mind, so that we might become Christ to one another and to the world.

In following the way of the Living Jesus, we place his vision and power at the center of our lives, and incarnate his mystic, healing, and prophetic spirit. We take on a new set of values and seek to "have the mind of Christ," embodied in embracing the profound interdependence of life and moving from individual self-interest to world loyalty. We embrace his Energy of Love to transform our lives and the world. We open to his all-encompassing and all-including vision; his love for the forgotten and marginalized; and his commitment to bring God's Vision to earth as it is in heaven. This is more than imitation of Christ, or the Way of Jesus, this is claiming the Living Jesus as our personal companion and inspiration for our own unique incarnation of God's love. The mind of Christ, described in Philippians 2, takes us beyond uniformity to uniqueness in which we become "fully alive" by living out our vocation to join our gifts with the world's needs. We become, to use the language of Martin Luther, "little Christs" by embracing and embodying our unique and emerging manifestation of the spirit of Jesus.

Lest it appear that the revival we need is concerned only with individual healing, process theology, following the ministry of Jesus, lives by the spirit of *ubuntu,* "I am because of you. We are because of each other." The whole universe conspires to create each moment of experience and each moment of experience shapes the universe beyond itself, nurturing or stalling the moral and spiritual arcs of history. Jesus breathed on his followers and said receive the Holy Spirit (John 20:21-23). The winds of the Spirit blew through individuals and also the gathered community and the world beyond. (Acts 2: 1-18). Jesus still breathes in us!

Process theology unites Infinite and finite, individual and community, and humankind and the planet. The spiritual formation of individuals enlivens communities and is nurtured by the communities of which we are a part. Just as persons are called to incarnate a personal relationship with Jesus, communities as also to be shaped by the gospel stories and openness to the Living Jesus. As the Apostle Paul affirms in 1 Corinthians 12, Christian community is a nursery for spiritual formation, and the actualizing of the gifts of each member bring health to the totality. The calling of Christian persons and communities is to bring forth the unique gifts of each person, regardless of race, ethnicity, nationality, age, sexuality, and intellectual achievement, for the glory of God and the healing of the planet.

With Jesus as our companion and guide, we and our communities of faith embrace interdependence, transformation, and healing. Trusting that "nothing can separate us from the love of God in Christ Jesus," we can face adversity on the long road to justice and environmental healing. (Romans 8:38-39) We become adventurers of ideas to change the world as we see Jesus in the "least of these" and hear whispers of his guidance everywhere. We incarnate the mystical vision of Jesus, seeing God's presence in everyone. We become his healing hands, channeling Jesus' healing energy, to bring wholeness to persons, communities, and the planet in "miraculous" ways. We claim our vocation as prophets recognizing that the Spirit of God enlivens us it did Jesus:

> to bring good news to the poor…
> to proclaim release to the captives
> and recovery of sight to the blind,
> to set free those who are oppressed,
> to proclaim the year of the Lord's favor. (Luke 4:18-19)

As Jesus' incarnations in our world, we heal cells, souls, cities, and civilizations, and bring forth God's Shalom on earth as it is in heaven.

Embodying the Living Jesus as our deepest reality, we experience his personal and transformational companionship and become his partners in healing the world. We come alive as members of lively congregations. As the panexperientialist mystic, bible scholar, organist, and physician, Albert Schweitzer asserts:

He comes to us as One unknown, without a name, as of old, by the lakeside, He came to those men who knew Him not. He speaks to us the same words: "Follow thou me!" and sets us to the tasks which He has to fulfill for our time. He commands. And to those who obey Him, whether they be wise or simple, He will reveal himself in the toils, the conflicts, the sufferings which they shall pass through in His fellowship, and, as an ineffable mystery, they shall learn in their own experience Who He is.[10]

GETTING PERSONAL WITH JESUS

Process theology affirms the ubiquitous presence of God. God is Ultimate Empath and Intimate Inspirer, the fellow sufferer who understands and the joyful companion who celebrates. God is the Alpha and Omega of each moment of experience providing each moment of experience with a vision of what it can become for itself and the world and providing energy of self-realization, and then receiving each moment as part of God's ongoing experience of the universe and the material from which God provides future possibilities for creative transformation. We can tap into possibility, energy, and intimacy through spiritual practices, which enable us to embody more fully the Divine Energy of Love incarnate in Jesus of Nazareth and ourselves.

Visualizing Jesus. The parent of the Society of Jesus, the Jesuits, Ignatius of Loyola developed a form of aesthetic spirituality in which you place yourself within a biblical story, seeing, feeling, smelling, hearing, and tasting, God's intimate presence and discovering that you are part of God's story of grace and healing. In a process-relational version Ignatius' "spiritual exercises," begin with a time of silence, awakening to God's presence, grace, and blessings in your life and in the world. Next, read a particular scripture passage twice, as if it is addressed personally to you. After a few moments of silence, imaginatively place yourself in the scriptural event, whether as an observer or participant. Visualize the scene, persons involved, Jesus, and the part you play, if any. Become a

---

10 Albert Schweitzer, *Albert Schweitzer: The Essential Writings* (Maryknoll, NY: Orbis Books, 2005), 41.

participant in the drama of incarnation and healing. Conclude this spiritual practice with a prayer of thanksgiving and openness to God's future presence in your life.

While you can choose a biblical scene, from either Testament, let me suggest a few in which Jesus is center stage.

- The woman with the flow of blood. (Mark 5:25-33)
- Zacchaeus the Tax Collector. (Luke 19:1-10)
- Mary of Magdala in the Garden with the Risen Jesus. (John 20:11-18)
- The boy with five loaves and two fish. (Matthew 14:13-21)
- The storm at sea. (Mark 4:35-41)
- The healing of sight impaired Bartimaeus. (Mark 10:46-52)
- The women receiving the great commission. (Matthew 28:1-10)

Asking for Guidance. Jesus is the archetype of alignment and unity with God's vision. Jesus sought to embody God's realm on earth as it is in heaven and lived in accordance with God's vision even in times of conflict. Charles Sheldon's *In His Steps*, a classic in the social gospel movement, charts the experience of persons who seek to be in alignment with the moral and spiritual arcs of the universe, embodied in the life and teachings of Jesus. After being convicted by his lack of compassion toward an unemployed man, pastor Henry Maxwell challenges his congregation with the following mandate, "Do not do anything without first asking, 'What would Jesus do?'"

In this spiritual practice, "ask, seek, knock" for insight into Jesus' presence and calling in your life. You might choose to frame this practice prayerfully with the following:

- Upon awakening, ask God/Jesus to reveal the divine presence to you in throughout your day.
- Ask "what would Jesus do?" in your decision-making and encounters.
- Seek to follow the wisdom you receive for your decisions and relationships.

21

Asking "what would Jesus do?" encourages mindfulness of God's presence and inspiration, reminding you that God is addressing you in every situation with possibilities for healing, justice-seeking, self-awareness, and spiritual growth. As Whitehead asserts, "God confronts the actual with what is possible for it… Every act leaves the world with a deeper or fainter impress of God. He then passes in his next relationship to the world with enlarged, or diminished, presentation of ideal values."[11]

Kything with Jesus. Author Madeleine L'Engle discovered the term "kything" in an old Scottish dictionary, belonging to her grandfather, and uses the term in her Time Trilogy books. Kything is a form of paranormal communication in which we join with another, sharing their thoughts, supporting their journey, and seeing the world through their eyes. An intimate prayer form, joining intercession and guidance, kything can be used to pray for another or communicate your love telepathically.[12] In recent years, I have used kything as a way of encountering Jesus or persons in need, usually on my predawn walks. In my practice, I take the following steps, which can also be used for connecting with another person in a holy way:

- Breathing deeply, I invoke the words of a gospel hymn, "I want Jesus to walk with me."
- Then, I visualize Jesus as my companion, walking beside me, sometimes holding hands or with arms over each other's shoulders.
- While I may simply enjoy the presence of Jesus, at certain times I engage in a conversation, asking for guidance, strength or course.
- In conclude by affirming that Jesus' promise to his disciples is made to me as well, "And, remember, I am with you always to the end of the age." (Matthew 28:20)

11 Alfred North Whitehead, *Religion in the Making* (New York: Macmillan, 1926), 149, 153, 152.
12 Louis Savary and Patricia Berne, *Kything: The Art of Spiritual Presence* (Mahweh, NJ: Paulist, 1989).

22

Loving Companion, let me know that you always walk beside me, giving me insight, courage, and strength. Help me to walk in your way and live out my agency and in ways that bring beauty and healing to the world you love. In Jesus' name Amen.

CHAPTER THREE

CHARISMATIC COSMOPOLITANISM

There's a wideness in God's mercy,
Like the wideness of the sea;
There's a kindness in God's justice,
Which is more than liberty.
But we make God's love too narrow
By false limits of our own,
And we magnify its strictness
With a zeal God will not own.
For the love of God is broader
Than the measures of the mind,
And the heart of the Eternal
Is most wonderfully kind.[13]

> By size I mean the stature of a person's soul, the range and depth of his love, his capacity for relationships… the volume of life you can take into your being and still maintain your integrity and individuality, the intensity and variety of outlook you can entertain in the unity of your being without feeling defensive or insecure… the strength of your spirit to encourage others to become freer in the development of their diversity and uniqueness.[14]

My friends often raise their eyebrows when I express concern at the news that a friend or a young adult reports, "I've found the Lord." "How could I, a Christian minister, not celebrate the return of a lost sheep to God's fold?" While I believe that authentic encounters with Jesus transform peoples' lives, I recognize that when someone claims they've become "saved," often their world becomes smaller. Their initial passion for Jesus becomes stifled by doctrinal and legalistic boundaries. Gradually, they begin to worry about the dangers of drag queens and homosexuality. Comments

---

13 Frederick William Faber, "There's a Wideness in Gods Mercy." (1862)
14 Harry James Cargas and Bernard Lee, *Religious Experience and Process Theology*. Mahweh, NJ: PaulistPress. 1976), 70.

about the threats transgender persons pose to children enter their vocabulary. They receive "inside" knowledge about who's saved and who isn't. As a young evangelical student declared to me, "My parents are good people, but they haven't accepted Jesus as their savior. If they were to die today, they would spend eternity in hell along with Gandhi and a lot of other good people." When I shared my universalist approach to salvation and revelation, she retorted, "If you don't believe in hell, you won't be saved either."

When the Jesus Movement of the sixties found Jesus, many idealistic young Christians discovered that the simple personal relationship with Jesus was encumbered by narrow creeds definitive of "true" Christianity. Indeed, today, in some quarters, there may even be a political litmus test separating the true believer from the secular world. Conservative Christianity has become the bastion of the Republican party, apart from which the GOP would have virtually no chance of winning elections. In the 2020 Presidential election, 85% of white evangelicals voted for Donald Trump, despite his incivility, hostility toward diversity, traumatizing of immigrant children, lack of any knowledge of Christianity, and failure to exhibit any of the gifts and graces extolled by Jesus' Sermon on the Mount.[15] Passion for Trump and his clones has superseded loyalty Jesus in intensity and salvific power.

A Bigger Piece of Jesus. During my final fulltime pastorate at an historic congregation on Cape Cod, Massachusetts, we regularly celebrated communion with a common loaf and cup. As people came to the communion table, they often struggled to tear off a miniscule piece of communion bread. To their surprise and occasional hilarity, I often whispered, "Why not take a bigger piece of Jesus. There's enough Jesus to go around." God wants us to have abundant life and that we can think big, act big, and accept the big-spirited grace of God. Nourished by a big piece of Jesus, we can expect great things from God and great things from ourselves.

Conservative evangelicals and progressive Christians need to partake in a bigger piece of Jesus. Conservative Christians need to liberate Jesus from biblical literalism, dogmatic creedalism, and ecclesiastical authoritarianism. Jesus is bigger than Christianity. The

15 "Most White Americans who regularly attend worship services voted for Trump in 2020" | Pew Research Center

true light of God enlightens everyone, regardless of culture, gender, sexuality, nation of origin, belief or unbelief, or religious tradition. A bigger piece of Jesus means widening the circle of inspiration and salvation so that God might be "all in all."

Progressives need to deepen their experience of God's presence and power. Our circles of salvation widen as we proclaim that the world lives by the incarnation of God, the reality "in whom we live and move and have our being." (Acts 17:28) Despite our aspiration to be inclusive, welcoming, and non-dual in our theology, we have often been God's "frozen chosen," failing to recognize the inherent mysticism, grounded in the incarnational spirit, of process and progressive theologies. We have been too rationalistic, too careful, and too afraid of being seen as heavenly-minded or mystically peculiar. We have forgotten that every religious tradition finds its initial energy from mystical experiences: Moses and the Burning Bush, Isaiah in the Temple, Mary and the angelic visitor, Jesus in the wilderness, Mary Magdala in the Garden, the fire and wind of Pentecost, Paul going to Damascus, Peter dreaming of a divine smorgasbord. We have been worried about mystical experiences undermining the rational mind. We chuckle at a joke attributed to Lily Tomlin, "When you speak to God, it's prayer. When God speaks to you, they call you crazy!" knowing her humor reflects our own biases. In contrast, a lively process and progressive Christianity needs to dance, sing, and shout "Hallelujah, and raise our hands. We need to meditate and march and pray and protest.

In the context of the "What if" question related to integrating the Jesus Movement with progressive Christians, I believe that process theology is large enough to embrace visionary experiences of God, speaking tongues, healing services, emotional encounters with Jesus, life-transforming dreams, near-death experiences, telepathy, and encounters with angelic beings. These experiences don't have to draw us away from the world's needs. They can be integrated with a rational and thoughtful faith. We need to remember that the prophetic encounter God drives us into the marketplace and awakens us to the cries of the poor and oppressed. We can be contemplative activists, Pentecostal protesters, evangelical-spirited ecologists, and mystical movement leaders.

Christ for the Community and Cosmos. Reclaiming the process-relational revival we need has opened up the gates of my childhood memories. In my own process of claiming the fullness of my personal religious history, hymns of my evangelical childhood have surfaced from my unconscious, enriching me as I understand them in universalist rather exclusivist ways. I now claim the evangelical spirit of relationship with Jesus, the fire and wind of Pentecost, and the importance of witness or faith sharing while affirming a wideness in God's mercy and God's global inspiration. A Jesus-inspired cosmopolitan spirituality gives new meaning to a revival hymn from childhood:

> Christ for the world we sing,
> the world to Christ we bring,
> with loving zeal;
> the poor, and them that mourn,
> the faint and overborne,
> sin-sick and sorrow-worn,
> whom Christ doth heal.

I understand this hymn differently than the evangelical Christians of my childhood Baptist church, who defined the world in terms of saved and unsaved, and believed that apart from a personal relationship with Jesus, there could be no salvation and companionship with Jesus after death. Colonialist and paternalistic in spirit, this hymn was intended to inspire unilateral evangelism, to the "lost" in our small Salinas Valley town and to those plunged in darkness in Africa and Asia. I now understand this hymn as involving open-spirited give-and-take witnessing, humble healing, and service-oriented hospitality, in a world where everyone is touched by God's grace. I believe there is a place where universalism and faith sharing meet, a place of relational sharing in which all conversation partners are enriched, and faith sharing is about partnership, justice-seeking, healing, and awakening, and not unilateral witnessing.

Today, the words "hybrid spirituality," "deep pluralism," and "inter-spirituality" are invoked in progressive Christian circles. Many progressive Christians use spiritual practices from other faith

27

traditions, such as mindfulness meditation, Tai Chi, Qigong, and energy work. I have been enriched by the integration of Christian and non-Christian practices. I returned to church, inspired by learning Transcendental Meditation. TM opened the door to Christian mysticism. My interest in the healings of Jesus and Christian healing practices resulted from learning Reiki healing touch. From the new age movement, I learned the healing power of affirmations, and discovered the Bible as a book of positive affirmations. My study of the First Testament prophets shaped my commitment to social justice and the prophetic spirit of Jesus. Celtic paganism and Christianity gave me a new appreciation of God's presence in the earth and its seasons. Integrating Christian spirituality with the wisdom of other faith traditions strengthens, not weakens, our commitment to the way of Jesus.

Process-relational theology inspires positive and creative give and take with other religions traditions. Faithfulness to the ever-present, ever-active, ever-inspiring God enables us to affirm that wherever truth, wisdom, and healing are present, God is its source, whether in a Zen monastery, Pagan seasonal ritual, Sufi dance, "secular" novel, medical laboratory, or mountaintop observatory. God is the ever-expanding spiral of creativity, who also centers all things. Centering in the way of Jesus, we can touch the centers of other religious traditions with appreciation and openness. The Way of Jesus that excludes no truthful way shines more brightly and our own faith's circle expands to embrace the wisdom of this good earth. Revival fires burst forth in experiencing God in Jesus and his companions in the world's faith traditions.

CULTIVATING A COSMOPOLITAN SPIRIT

To be "cosmopolitan" means to make the whole world your community. Cosmopolitan spirituality welcomes diversity and novelty and sees "otherness" as an opportunity for the cultivation of growth and wisdom. In fact, for the spirit-centered cosmopolitan Christian, there is no "other." We are one in the Spirit, as God's beloved children, despite our amazing and bountiful diversity. Inspired by Nicholas of Cusa and Bonaventure, we will live out the meaning of "God is the circle whose center is everywhere and whose circumference is nowhere."

Living from the Center.16 Deep down we are always centered in God, even when we forget our center or become de-centered as a result of anxiety and misplaced values. In this practice, gently inhale and exhale. With each breath, focus your attention on the Spirit of Jesus within. Experience yourself as calm and compassionate, and centered in the Divine in yourself, whether by yourself or in a worship community embodying Jesus' vision and power in mind, body, and spirit.

Widening the Circle. In this exercise, begin with centering breaths. As you inhale, feel the universe energizing and enlightening you. You are supported by Life in all its diversity. You are the light of the world. Let your light shine. Now as you exhale, experience your breath joining the breath of creation in all its variety. Let the Holy Breath of the Universe join you with all things.

The Elephant is Running and We can Run with It. The ancient story of the sight impaired persons and the elephant needs to be updated for our twenty-first century pluralistic age. While each tradition focuses on certain aspects of the divine elephant, a living elephant never stands still. It is breathing, walking, running, waving its ears, and making noise. As the divine elephant moves, living faith evolves, discovering new aspects of the Holy and expanding its vision of the Divine in encountering other faiths. In this exercise, reflect on your understanding of the Holy. How would you describe the divine elephant? What aspects of the divine elephant do you emphasize in your spiritual journey? What aspects are emphasized in your faith community? Then, widen your vision, considering: What aspects of the divine elephant might you be neglecting? How might you grow toward greater stature in understanding of the Holy? What might you, or your congregation, learn from other faith traditions that would deepen your faith as a progressive, process-relational Christian?

God of Change and Glory, thank you for the varieties of spiritual experience. Thank you for human and cultural

16 This section's title is inspired by Jay McDaniel's book, *Living from the Center* (St. Louis: Chalice Press, 2000).

diversity. Let me see diversity and pluralism as a blessing and commit myself to spiritual growth, recognizing that despite the diversity of life, there is truly no other. In the Spirit of Divine Artistry and Adventure. Amen.

CHAPTER FOUR

WHY NOT BECOME FIRE?

Every time I feel the spirit moving in my heart,
I will pray.

> God is thus at once the source of novelty and the lure to
> finer and richer actualizations embodying that novelty. Thus
> God is the One who calls us beyond all that we have become
> to what might be.[17]

A story from the African Desert Parents describes the encounter
between Abba Lot and Abba Joseph that highlights the challenges
facing process-relational and progressive Christianity. One day
Abba Lot visited the venerable Abba Joseph in search of spiritual
guidance. Abba Lot confessed to the elder, "Abba Joseph, as far as
I can, I say my daily office, fast, pray, and meditate. I live in peace
and as far as I'm able purify my thoughts. What more can I do?"
In response, the elder stretched his hands toward heaven, with his
fingers blazing, and exclaimed, "Why not become fire?"

To embody a passionate faith that transforms our lives, congregations, and the world is our challenge today. "God is still
speaking," so affirms a United Church of Christ motto, provoking
the question, "Is anyone listening?" Process theology proclaims a
God-filled world in which God addresses us in every moment of
experience and every encounter. There are burning bushes, Damascus roads, and Garden voices everywhere. We are always receiving
divine guidance and the energy to actualize divine possibilities.

Dorothee Sölle announces, "We are all mystics" and we should
do all we can personally, congregationally, and politically to encour-
age mystical experiences. We need to live our theology. We need to
embrace a beautiful and passionate God and the healer and prophet
Jesus and become fire in our personal and communal spiritualities
and social activism.

---

17 John B. Cobb, *God and the World* (Philadelphia: Westminster/John Knox,
1969), 82.

The Jesus movement of the sixties was grounded in mystical experiences of the living Jesus as companion and friend. The Asbury Revival found its inspiration in the quest for a personal experience of Jesus. Yet, these idealistic Christians often affiliate with churches that are suspicious of mysticism, believing that God can best be found in only through the words of scripture and religious authorities, counseling an individualistic relationship with Jesus and judgment of those who follow different paths or fall outside their norms of sexuality or lifestyle. Meditation is still viewed with concern in conservative evangelical circles, as circumventing the biblical Jesus and inerrant scripture, and becoming an entry way to heretical religious hospitality and affirmation of spiritualities of indigenous and global religions. Yet, as Jesus said to Nicodemus, "The wind blows where it chooses, and you hear the sound of it, but you do not know where it comes from or where it goes. So it is with everyone who is born of the Spirit." (John 3:8-10) The freedom of God's Spirit threatens every orthodoxy, fundamentalism, and institutional authoritarianism.

In contrast to conservative Christianity, progressive Christianity affirms spiritual freedom, but often fails to connect persons and communities to the animating Spirit of Jesus and mystics and spirit persons throughout the ages. The Whiteheadian century David Griffin anticipated must join head, heart, and hands. Transformative theology must be joined with lively spiritual practices and fiery experiences of the Holy and an equally passionate quest to be God's companions in healing the world.

Passionate Process Practices. Transformative faith involves the interplay of vision, promise, and practice. The *process-relational vision* describes a dynamic, interdependent, panexperiential, and open-ended universe in which God is moving through our personal and corporate lives and inviting us to be agents of creative transformation in the historical process. The whole earth is full of God's glory as we discover:

All nature sings and round me rings
The music of the spheres…

God shines in all that's fair
In the rustling grass I hear God pass
God speaks to me everywhere.

God's "spirit of gentleness," described by Jim Manley, is also the movement of restlessness, challenging our institutions, communities, and nations to "let justice roll down like waters and righteousness like an ever-flowing stream" (Amos 5:24).

The *process-relational promise* is that we can experience the God-filled, God-inspired world described by theologians. At the depth of each moment of experience, God's grace and possibility abound. We don't need to go anywhere to experience God. The world lives by the incarnation of God – in us! We can live process theology by attentiveness to God's presence in every experience and encounter and openness to the paranormal, immanent, unconscious, and ever-present inspiration of God in our lives.

While *process-relational practices* share much in common with the varieties of global spiritual practice, process spirituality integrates conscious and unconscious, transcendent and immanent, spirit and body, *kataphatic* images and *apophatic* dazzling darkness, and contemplation and activism. The way in is the way out, and the outer activism inspires inner reflection. The world of process-relational spirituality prizes both contemplation and action and sees them as intimately and dynamically interdependent. Inspired by their encounter with God and companionship with Jesus, the progressive mystic wants everyone to experience the democracy of the Spirit. This leads to confronting every institutional structure that stands in the way of experiencing abundant life.

COMMUNICATION IS EVERYTHING.

The revival we need depends on communication. Process theology needs to be expressed in ways that communicate its vision of God, human existence, and the non-human world to lay persons. If process theology remains the domain of scholastics, its impact will be minimal. We need to convey process theology, spirituality, and social responsibility with minimal jargon and maximal concreteness. We need to transform the language of Whitehead –

prehensions, concrescence, initial aims, primordial and consequent natures of God – to speak to the hearts and minds of children as well as adults. Academics and seminarians need to privilege praxis, the practical application of process theology for theological reflection, spiritual growth, and social and planetary activism. This is not just a problem for process theology. George Bernard Shaw said that "the professions are a conspiracy against laypeople." Many pastors and spiritual leaders never learn to convey their seminary insights to lay audiences. How often do you hear of mainline and progressive congregations having courses in church history, theological ethics, theology, spirituality, or even bible? We must be able live and breathe process theology for it to make a difference in today's world.[18] We need to teach pastors and professors how to teach process theology and connect it with current social and ethical issues to revive the mind and spirit of the church. This is truly the work of head, heart, and hands, of spiritually awakened people and vibrant and committed communities, inspired to heal the planet.

PRACTICING AND PROCLAIMING PASSIONATE PROCESS THEOLOGY

Whitehead invokes terms like zest, intensity of experience, beauty, peace, creativity and adventure to describe what it means to be fully alive personally and institutionally. Whitehead would have appreciated Howard Thurman's counsel, "Don't ask what the world needs. Ask what makes you come alive, and go do it. Because what the world needs is people who have come alive." If theology and spirituality do not make our communities and persons come alive, there is little hope that we can change the world. While we might have questions about the staying power and ultimate goals of the Asbury Revival and its predecessor, the Jesus Movement of the sixties and seventies, we must admit that for a brief moment in time, their participants were "alive." They found meaning, purpose, and healing. For process-relational revivalists, the quest for mean-

18 Process and Faith, Open Horizons, and the Energion Topical Line Drives Series, featuring books by John Cobb and Jay McDaniel, Patricia Adams Farmer, Ron Farmer, and myself are initiatives in making process theology come alive for laypersons.

ing, purpose, and healing must be global as well as individual, and it must enlarge rather than constrict our sense of hospitality and affirmation of pluralism. We need to find ways to share inclusive mystical and theological visions to those who have experienced themselves touched by God in lively ways, whether college students, weary parents, or active senior adults.

Sensational Spirituality. The ever-present and ever-loving God can be found everywhere and in all things. This first practice is purely sensational. Open your senses to the world. Taste and see the goodness of God. Listen for the harmony of the spheres. Touch the incarnation in walking barefoot, petting a companion animal, or hugging a child, friend, or life companion. Smell the roses, rosemary, sea air, or morning freshness. Rejoice and give thanks for God who comes to you in all things.

A variation of this involves taking time to read Psalm 148 and its description of a world of praise quietly. Let the images of lively, interdependent, sacred reality fill your heart and mind. Meditate on the images of God praised by the sun, moon, and stars, snow and ice, whales and sharks, pangolins, sparrows, eagles, and humankind.

As you delight in the living, praising universe, ask God to reveal ways that you can support the healing of the earth, beginning with your daily life and expanding to your social responsibility.

Passionate Spirituality. Although Howard Thurman was a contemplative activist, and inspiration to Martin Luther King, he counsels us to "ask what makes you come alive, and go do it."

In this spiritual practice, after a time of silence, ask for divine guidance and insight into the following questions: What feeds your spirit? When do you feel God's pleasure? When makes you feel most alive?

Remembering that the "glory of God is a fully alive person," awaken to Divine Energy and Possibility flowing in and through you, enlivening you and energizing others. Look for ways to join your inner passion, your spiritual giftedness, with the wellbeing and healing of those around you, your congregation and community, and nation and planet. Come alive and then do it!

Amazing and Beautiful God, fill my senses with beauty and wonder. Help me delight in flora and fauna, and sea and sky. Let every breath be a blessing, filling me with the energy of the Spirit and inspiring me to breathe new life into the world around me. In gratitude to the Spirit. Amen.

CHAPTER FIVE

A MOVING IMAGE OF ETERNITY

Strength for today and bright hope for tomorrow
Blessings all mine with ten thousand beside.[19]

An insistent craving – the insistent craving that zest for existence be refreshed by the ever-present, unfading importance of our immediate actions, which perish and yet live evermore.[20]

On the night my mother unexpectedly died, our ten-year-old son, unaware of her death, dreamed that our family was walking along the beach and my mother said to him, "Tell Everett, everything will be ok." Our son's experience reflects the growing cultural interest in survival after death and paranormal experiences to which process theologians must respond in terms of its creative theological vision. While once process thinkers, such as Charles Hartshorne, categorically denied survival after death, believing it to a form of selfishness, today process theologians and progressives are beginning to ponder near death experiences, telepathy, and precognition, and are open to the possibility that these experiences may point to a deeper naturalism in which the human spirit lives beyond physical death.

It is reasonable to ask, "what has everlasting life, or immortality, to do with revival?" Is interest in survival after death just an illusory add on to provide comfort for those who no longer anticipate a positive future for themselves or the planet? Or, does it revive a sense of hope that empowers us to see life as a holy adventure in which our actions to secure justice and heal the world are connected with God's vision of Shalom and companionship with God beyond the grave? Does it give hope and courage to invest ourselves in the future of our planet despite the fact that our planetary future is in doubt? I believe the answer must be "yes."

---

19 Thomas Chisholm, "Great is Thy Faithfulness" (1923).
20 Alfred North Whitehead, *Process and Reality: Corrected Edition* (New York: Free Press, 1979), 351.

Over the years, my interest in survival after death as a believer and theologian has increased. Liberated from the transactional and individualistic understandings of heaven and hell taught in my childhood church, I now ponder a vision of everlasting life that affirms this life while imagining spiritual evolution beyond this lifetime.

The possibility of everlasting life and communion with "good ancestors" of the past shaped the writing of this text. After my closest spiritual friend died several years ago, I began asking her for wisdom in my writing, teaching, and preaching. Over the years, I have included other "good ancestors," including my parents and brother, teachers, pastoral mentors, and recently David Griffin in my prayers for wisdom. I believe I have received subtle communications and inspirations from the "saints" of my life. While I don't claim to know if these prayers or connections make a literal difference, I believe the very process of opening to the influence of "deceased" companions opens up the unconscious mind to greater wisdom or connects me to their wisdom on earth and in the afterlife.

I also ask the living and risen Jesus to guide my writing, teaching, and preaching, as well as personal decisions, so that I might give glory to God and support the healing of the earth. I have come to believe that if there is an afterlife, our ancestors' love is more expansive than it was in this lifetime. I also believe that the interdependence of the universe not only connects us with the past and present but may even join us with those whom we describe as deceased.

Although process theology remains agnostic as to the precise nature of the afterlife, it is open to the afterlife as a continuing holy adventure of spiritual and relational evolution in which hope for everlasting life encourages, rather than discourages, concern for issues of justice and earth care in this world.

Process theology sees this life and the afterlife as interrelated. Immortality is both objective and subjective. We shape our own and others' experiences by our behaviors today. Time is the moving image of eternity, in which our lives reflect the presence of divine providence and possibility and contribute to the ongoing evolution of this world. Our lives perish, moment by moment and as a stream of experiences, and yet live evermore. Our survival is "objective" in its impact in this lifetime and in the evolving memory of God. The good we do lasts forever and supports the realization of God's vision on earth as it is in heaven. If personal identity exists beyond the grave, we are shaping our own and other persons' everlasting life by our actions today. What we do now has consequences in this life and the next.

Survival after death, from a process perspective, gives us hope and courage to face the personal and planetary challenges of this lifetime. We don't have to wait for heaven to experience God. God is already touching our lives each moment in our personal and political decision-making and inviting us to incarnate God's vision in this world. When Dorothy Day, the mystical activist and parent of the Catholic Worker movement said that she spoke to persons as if they were angels, she meant that we look for the divine and eternal in everyone we meet and treat them as eternal spirits.

Progressive Christians have often abandoned life-affirming images of survival after death as a way of repudiating the transactional, exclusivist, and in-and-out group images of heaven and hell of conservative Christianity. We have focused on what we don't believe than positive images of the relationship of this life and the next. We can have a robust universalism that describes life as a holy adventure, a pilgrimage toward self-realization and Christ-companionship in both this lifetime and beyond. Rather than turning us away from the world, images of survival after death in terms of ongoing spiritual growth inspire concern for this world. Every creature we meet enjoys "objective immortality" in God's memory and may also partake in God's everlasting life. Beloved by God, they deserve our love in this holy here and now. Recognizing God's stake in this world and in every creature right now, our calling is to live fully in the present, doing something beautiful for God's creation, knowing our love continues to live on God. I believe seeing our lives as part of an everlasting adventure enchants this world, promotes openness to mystical experiences, and revives our sense of the wonder of each moment as the meeting place of time and eternity.

Images of survival after death join justice now with ultimate justice in everlasting life. There is much tragedy in this life. Many persons are brutalized, live with unendurable pain, and are the victims of personal and political violence. The injustices and traumatic experiences of this life cry out for healing and for us to embody God's love for the "least of these." They inspire the dream of another realm where pain is relieved, injustice overcome, imagination freed, and persons realize their full potential as God's beloved children in God's ongoing Beloved Community.[21]

There is revival, healing, and creative transformation for all of us – the youthful college student, an "in the closet" hippie preacher, an erudite theologian, and a forgotten child. Process theology inspires a holy adventure with Jesus as our companion, God as our inspiration, the Spirit as our passion, the whole world as a sanctuary for healing and community, and a lively evolving, healing, and all-embracing future awaiting us all. This is a gospel worth proclaiming and a revival we need.

PRACTICING EVERLASTING LIFE

Time is the moving image of eternity in which each moment perishes and lives evermore in God's memory and its impact on the universe. Process theology is a resource in overcoming the dualism of the seen and unseen and this life and the next. In this spiritual exercise, visualize God's presence in your life, experiencing Jesus as your deepest reality. Christ is in you, guiding you and joining this life and the next. Moving beyond yourself, visualize God's presence in a companion's life. See the holiness at the heart of their lives. Now, visualize the face of stranger, perhaps, from a different ethic, national, gender, sexual, or political identity. See the holiness in their lives.

---

21 I am agnostic about what characteristics qualify a creature for everlasting life. All creation, from the simplest to most complex, contributes to God's experience – the divine memory - and the ongoing history of our world, and has "objective immortality." Whether non-human creatures, with complex nervous systems, survive death in some way or are carried into the next life by the mutuality of our love, is a possibility. A God who loves the world must surely want fulfillment or peace for everything that exists.

Commit yourself to honoring the divine in yours and every life. In the spirit of Dorothy Day, make a commitment to speak to everyone as if they are an angel. Bring beauty to their lives, knowing that your acts of kindness, compassion, justice-seeking, and beauty-making endure forever and shape the future of those with whom you interact. Ponder the everlasting consequences of bringing beauty and love to your relationships and the world.

Everlasting Companion, let me join time and eternity in every action. Let me see the angelic in every creature and commit myself to doing something beautiful for God in every encounter. Let me experience "strength for today and bright hope for tomorrow" with "blessings all mine and ten thousand beside" In the name of Jesus the Living One. Amen.

BOOKS FOR THE REVIVAL WE NEED

John Cobb, *Christ in a Pluralistic Age* (Westminster/John Knox, 1975).

John Cobb and Jay McDaniel, *Choosing Life: Ecological Civilization as the World's Best Hope* (Energion, 2020).

Monica Coleman, *Making a Way When There is Now Way: A Womanist Theology* (Fortress, 2008).

Bruce Epperly, *Healing Marks: Healing and Spirituality in Mark's Gospel* (Energion, 2012).

Bruce Epperly, *Process Spirituality: Practicing Holy Adventure* (Energion, 2017).

Bruce Epperly, *Process Theology: A Guide for the Perplexed* (Continuum, 2011).

Bruce Epperly, *Process Theology: Embracing Adventure with God* (Energion, 2104).

Bruce Epperly, *Taking a Walk with Whitehead* (Energion, 2023)

Bruce Epperly, *The Elephant is Running: Process and Open and Relational Theologies and Religious Pluralism* (SacraSage, 2022).

Bruce Epperly, *Transforming Acts: Acts of Apostles as a Twenty-first Century Gospel* (Energion, 2013).

Patricia Adams Farmer, *Beauty and Process Theology: A Journey of Transformation* (Energion, 2020).

Patricia Adams Farmer, *Embracing a Beautiful God* (Chalice, 2003).

Sheri Kling, *A Process Spirituality: Christian and Transreligious Resources for Transformation* (Lexington, 2020).

Jay McDaniel, *Living from the Center* (Chalice, 2000).

Marjorie Suchocki, *In God's Presence* (Chalice, 1996).

Topical Line Drives

Straight to the point in 44 pages
https://topicallinedrives.com